Seeds of Faith

I Believe

Karissa Jekel / Subi

I believe every morning
is like an empty page,
waiting to be coloured in
by someone just like me.

I believe the sun will rise
to say hello when I wake up.
I colour my page orange and gold,
bright and shining.

I believe my mommy will greet me
with a warm hug.
I colour my page pink
to show her my love.

I believe in sharing.
The circle of giving never ends.
I colour my page yellow,
like some of my favourite flowers.

I believe in laughter.
Laughing can cure almost anything!
I colour my page purple,
like the bandage on my knee.

I believe in happiness.
Just look around and listen –
happiness is never far away.
I colour my page bright blue,
like the sky and the sea.

I believe in prayer.
Every day I spend time talking to God.
I colour my page with golden light,
God's light shining in my heart.

I believe God cares for me,
for God is a light for my path.
I colour my page green,
because my path is full of life.

I believe in God's love for all of us.
In the Bible, a rainbow
was a sign of God's promise
to Noah and to all of us.
I colour my page with rainbows,
because they are beautiful!

I believe in God's Spirit of love,
a light that leads the way.
I colour my page yellow
to light up the world.

I believe in dreaming.
I close my eyes and imagine...

I colour my page silver and white,
then in my mind I soar on feathery wings.

I believe God fills my world
with joy and light
so I can add colour
to everything I see!

I believe you can colour
each new day, too.
Go ahead and use the
colours God gives you!

Activity

I Believe!

For this activity you will need:
- 1 small jar and lid
- coloured paper
- scissors
- 10 small pieces of paper to write or draw on
- crayons, coloured pencils or markers
- tape
- stickers

Step 1: Cut a piece of coloured paper large enough to wrap around your jar.

Step 2: On the paper write these words in big letters: I BELIEVE!

Step 3: Carefully tape the paper around the jar.

Step 4: On the 10 small pieces of paper, write or draw some of the things you believe. (Read the book again to find some ideas.) Decorate the papers with happy colours.

Step 5: Fold up the papers and twist the ends so they look like wrapped candies, then put them inside the jar. Put the lid on the jar and decorate the lid with stickers.

Step 6: Share your beliefs with your family and talk about them together. Say a prayer together when you are finished to thank God for being with you every day!

Prayer

Dear God,

I believe you love me with all your heart.
I pray that I will always remember to love you
and share your love with others in what I say and do.
Watch over me and guide me every day of my life.
Amen.

Trust in the Lord with all your heart.
Proverbs 3:5

Originally published by Gemser Publications, Spain
Layout: Gemser Publications, S.L.
© Gemser Publications, S.L. 2011
El Castell, 38 08329 Teià (Barcelona, Spain)
www.mercedesros.com

This edition © 2012 Novalis Publishing Inc.
Cover design: Audrey Wells
Adaptation of text: Anne Louise Mahoney
Published by Novalis
www.novalis.ca

Novalis Publishing Office
10 Lower Spadina Avenue, Suite 400
Toronto, Ontario, Canada
M5V 2Z2

Head Office
4475 Frontenac Street
Montréal, Québec, Canada
H2H 2S2

Library and Archives Canada Cataloguing in Publication
      Jekel, Karissa
      I believe / Karissa Jekel ; Subi, illustrator.

      (Seeds of faith)
      ISBN 978-2-89646-476-0

      1. Faith--Juvenile literature. I. Subirana, Joan II. Title.
      III. Series: Jekel, Karissa. Seeds of faith.

      BV4637.J45 2012   j234'.23   C2012-901218-1

Printed in China.

We acknowledge the financial support of the Government of Canada through the Canada Book Fund for business development activities.

5   4   3   2   16   15